Nakshatra Van
Celestial Garden Plantation

Record of landscaping and plantation of 108 Trees having Medicinal and Divine attributes, related to the 27 Nakshatra Birth Stars

Ashwini Kumar Aggarwal

जय गुरुदेव

ISBN13: 978-93-48012-59-3 Paperback Edition
ISBN13: 978-93-48012-25-8 Hardbound Edition
ISBN13: 978-93-48012-94-4 Digital Edition

Title: **Nakshatra Van Celestial Garden Plantation**
Author: **Ashwini Kumar Aggarwal**

Printed and Published by
Devotees of Sri Sri Ravi Shankar Ashram

https://advaita56.weebly.com/   The Art of Living Centre
https://www.artofliving.org/

Devotees Library Cataloging-in-Publication Data
Aggarwal, Ashwini Kumar.
Language: English. Thema: PSAF WNJ VXFA 2ACB
BISAC: SCI020000 SCIENCE / Life Sciences / Ecology
Keywords: 1) Nakshatra Van. 2) Vedic Sacred Grove. 3) Birth Star Trees. 4) Astral Garden.
Typeset in 12 Source Sans Pro

21 April 2025 Sarvartha Siddhi Yoga, Shravana upari Uttara Ashadha Nakshatra, Ashtami Tithi, Krishna Paksha, Vaishakha Masa, Grishma Ritu, Uttarayana.
COMPLETION OF NAKSHATRA VAN 108 TREES PLANTATION AT SUNVIEW RESIDENCY.
19th April Engrossed in Jahnavi Harrison concert 7:15 – 9:45pm Indradhanush Auditorium. Supreme Bliss. Nectar of Krishna's Radha, Mirabai experienced.
20th April Excellent scientific discussions with Temple Sthapati.

Vikram Samvat 2082 Kalayukta, Saka Samvat 1947 Vishvavasu

1st Edition April 2025

जय गुरुदेव

Dedication

H H Sri Sri Ravi Shankar

who inspires us to protect and care for our planet Earth

Front Cover Image credits

Photo dated 21 April 2025, by Jagjit ji.

Acknowledgements

Entire methodology and precise plan given by most respected Sadhvi Hemswaroopa.

21st April 2025. After completion of plantation during the drive home, at 9:15am saw a happy Peacock on fence, busy pecking grains. Soon after saw a Mongoose scurrying across in Mahavir Enclave. Upon reaching home, at 9:30am, we celebrated in lobby with bhajan "Hari Sundar Nand Mukunda".

18th April 1:08pm Saw bull and cow adjacent to Patiala home. 22nd April brought bull and cow in Nakshatra Van for 15 days grazing.

Blessing

People should be encouraged to have reverence for the planet, to revere trees and rivers as sacred, to treat people as sacred, and to see God in Nature. This will foster sensitivity; and a sensitive person can't but care for nature and nurture the environment.

H H Sri Sri Ravi Shankar

World Environment Day, June 2018

During Gurudev's Ludhiana visit on 19th Feb, at 11:40am in Sunview office, he told us to plant a Nakshatra Van. At that time Sadhvi Hemswaroopa was present as the technical expert on such plantation, and we finally got inspired to make it.

TABLE OF CONTENTS

Prayer

ॐ भद्रं कर्णेभिश्र् श्रृणुयाम देवाः । भद्र पश्ये माक्षभिर् यजत्राः । स्थिरैरङ्गैस् तुष्टुवाᶍ सस्तनूभिः । व्यशेम देवहितयँ यदायुः । स्वस्ति न इन्द्रो वृद्धश्रवाः । स्वस्ति नᶍ पूषा विश्ववेदाः । स्वस्ति नस्ताक्ष्यों अरिष्टनेमिः । स्वस्ति नो बृहस्पतिर्दधातु ॥ ॐ शान्तिः शान्तिः शान्तिः ॥

oṃ bhadraṃ karṇebhiś śṛṇuyāma devāḥ | bhadra paśye

mākṣabhir yajatrāḥ | sthirairaṅgais tuṣṭuvāᶍ sastanūbhiḥ |

vyaśema devahitaym̐ yadāyuḥ | svasti na indro

vṛddhaśravāḥ | svasti naᶍ pūṣā viśvavedāḥ | svasti

nastārkṣyo ariṣṭanemiḥ | svasti no bṛhaspatirdadhātu ||

oṃ śāntiḥ śāntiḥ śāntiḥ ||

O Beloved Lord!
May my ears hear the auspicious, may my eyes admire the beauty around me...may all my senses be tuned to thy magnificent creation.

May you keep me aligned to the path by helping deepen my faith in all the Wonderful Beings on this Supremely Divine Planet Earth.

1st Day 25-03-2025 Shravan - Rui

PLANTATION DAY 1. Morning.
We sat on a chatai spread on the soft mud. The five of us in Bliss.

Date: Tuesday 25-03-2025, 7:45 – 9:15 am, Ekadashi Tithi.
Nakshatra Birth Star: 22. श्रवण Shravan = Altair
Constellation: Aquila

Sacred Tree Planted (4 nos):
रुई rui = milk weed = calotropis gigantea

Sacred Mantra: "oṃ śravaṇāya namaḥ".
Endowment given after Plantation: a **coconut** to a suitable person.

Rui Shrub. (offered during Hanuman worship).

2nd Day 26-03-2025 Dhanishtha - Shami

PLANTATION DAY 2. Morning.
We sat on a chatai spread on the soft mud. The five of us in Bliss.

Date: Wednesday 26-03-2025, 7:45 – 9:15 am, Dvadashi Tithi.
Nakshatra Birth Star: 23. धनिष्ठा Dhanishtha – β Delphini = Rotanev
Constellation: Delphinus

Sacred Tree Planted (4 nos):
शमी shami = persian mesquite = prosopis cineraria

Sacred Mantra – "oṃ dhaniṣṭhāyai namaḥ".
Endowment given after Plantation – he-goat (**billy**) to a shepherd.

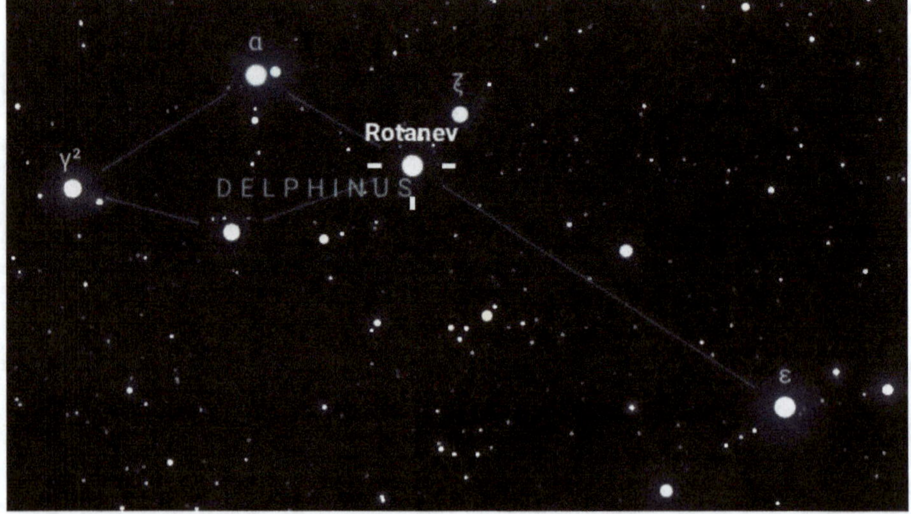

Shami Shrub

3rd Day 27-03-2025 Shatabhisha - Kadamb

PLANTATION DAY 3. Morning.
We sat on a chatai spread on the soft mud. The five of us in Bliss.

Date: Thursday 27-03-2025, 7:45 – 9:15 am, Trayodashi Tithi.
Nakshatra Birth Star: 24. शतभिषा (शततारका) Shatabhisha-Sadalmelik
Constellation: Aquarius (Zodiac).

Sacred Tree Planted (4 nos):
कदंब kadamb = bur flower – neolamarckia cadamba

Sacred Mantra – "oṃ śatabhiṣaje namaḥ".
Endowment given after Plantation - **lunch including jaggery** to office painter.

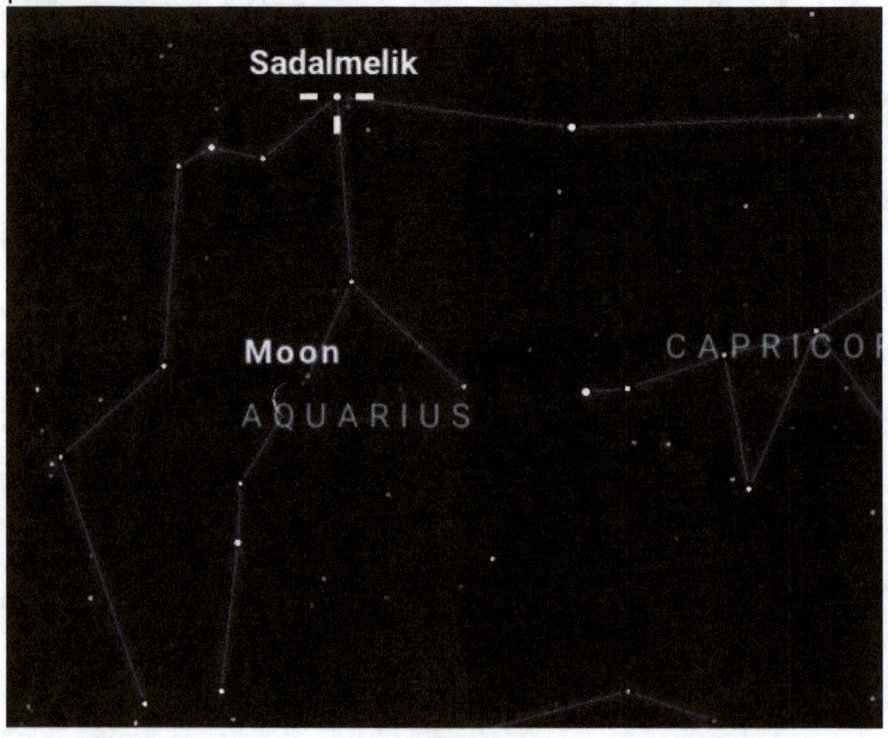

Kadamb

4th Day 28-03-2025 P. Bhadrapada - Mango

PLANTATION DAY 4. Morning. **We got our Quechua portable tent.**
Date: Friday 28-03-2025, 7:45 – 9:15 am, Chaturdashi Tithi.
Nakshatra Birth Star: 25. पूर्वा भाद्रपदा Purva Bhadrapada - Scheat
Constellation: Pegasus

Sacred Tree Planted (4 nos):
आम aam = mango - mangifera indica

Sacred Mantra – "oṃ pūrvāproṣṭhapadbhyāṃ namaḥ".

Endowment given after Plantation – gave **foodgrains** to a suitable person.

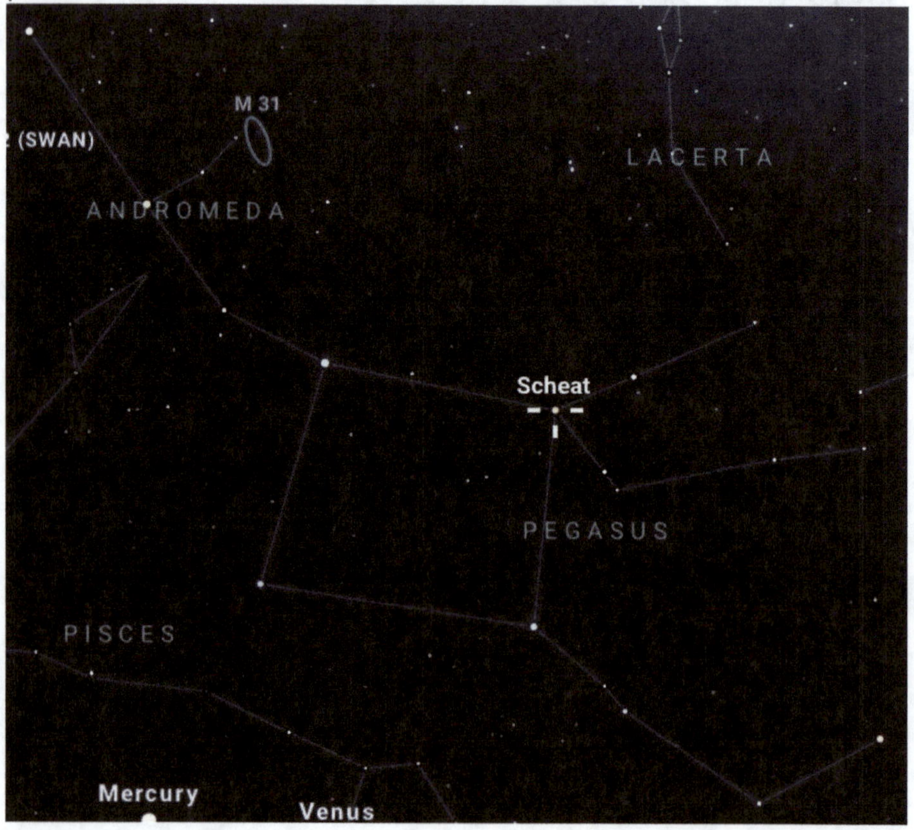

5th Day 29-03-2025 U. Bhadrapada - Neem

PLANTATION DAY 5. Morning.
Date: Saturday 29-03-2025, 7:45 – 9:15 am, Amavasya Tithi.
Nakshatra Birth Star: 26. उत्तरा भाद्रपदा Uttar Bhadrapada - Algenib
Constellation: Pegasus

Sacred Tree Planted (4 nos):
नीम neem = margosa - azadirachta indica

Sacred Mantra – "oṃ uttaraproṣṭhapadabhyāṃ namaḥ".

Endowment given after Plantation - fed **lunch** to a teammate of the office painter.

Neem Tree

6th Day 30-03-2025 Revati - Mahua

PLANTATION DAY 6. Morning.
Date: Sunday 30-03-2025, 7:45 – 9:15 am, Pratipada Tithi.
Nakshatra Birth Star: 27. रेवती Revati – Zeta Piscium
Constellation: Pisces (Zodiac).

Sacred Tree Planted (4 nos):

महुआ mahua = indian butter tree – madhuca longifolia

Sacred Mantra – "oṃ revatyai namaḥ".

Endowment given after Plantation – **educate**/gave Sri Sri's book to office manager.

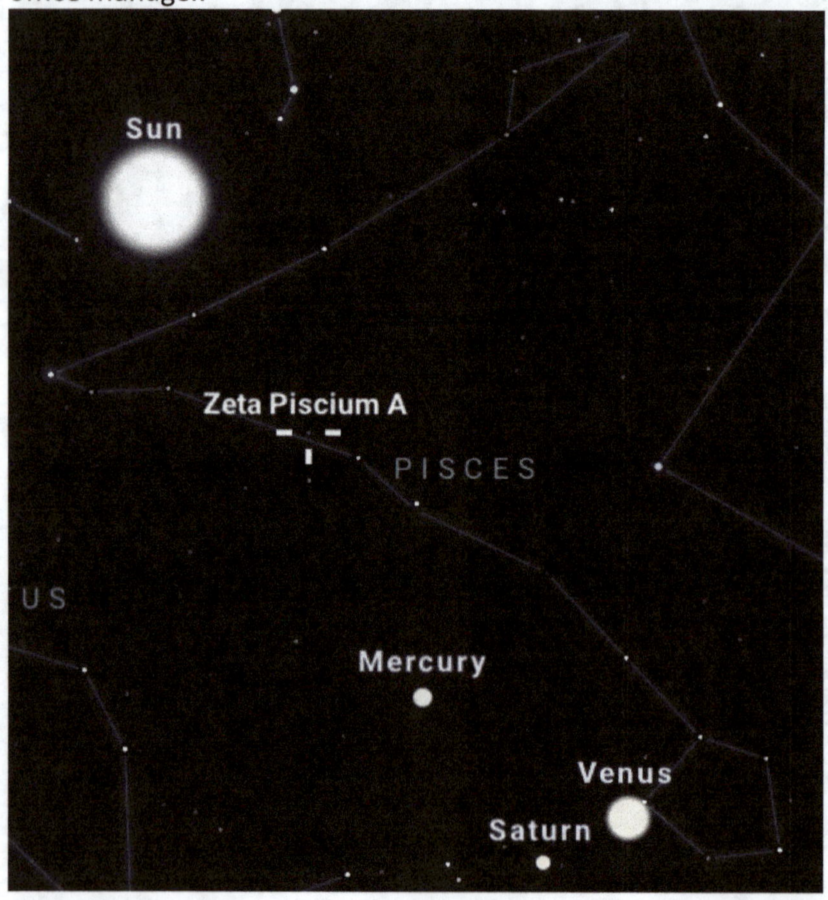

Mahua

7th Day 31-03-2025 Ashwini - Kuchala

PLANTATION DAY 7. Morning.
Date: Monday 31-03-2025, 7:45 – 9:15 am, Dvitiya Tithi.
Nakshatra Birth Star: 1. अश्विनी Ashwini - Beta Arietis = Sheratan
Constellation: Aries (Zodiac).

Sacred Tree Planted (4 nos):
जहर कुचला kuchala = poison nut - strychnos nux-vomica

Sacred Mantra – "oṃ aśvayugabhyāṃ namaḥ".
Endowment given after Plantation - fed **dinner** to a teammate of the office painter.

Kuchala Tree.

8th Day 1-04-2025 Bharani - Amla

PLANTATION DAY 8. Morning.
Date: Tuesday 1-04-2025, 7:45 – 9:15 am, Chaturthi Tithi.
Nakshatra Birth Star: 2. भरणी Bharani - 39 Arietis
Constellation: Aries (Zodiac).

Sacred Tree Planted (4 nos):
आंवला amla = Indian gooseberry – phyllanthus emblica

Sacred Mantra – "oṃ apabharaṇībhyo namaḥ".
Endowment given after Plantation - **fed the cows** in our goshala.

Amla in bloom.

9th Day 2-04-2025 Morning Krittika - Gular

PLANTATION DAY 9. Morning.
Date: Wednesday 2-04-2025, 7:45 – 9:15 am, Pancami Tithi.
Nakshatra Birth Star: 3. कृत्तिका Krittika - Pleiades
Open Cluster: Pleiades.

Sacred Tree Planted (4 nos):
गूलर gular = cluster fig – ficus racemosa

Sacred Mantra – "oṃ kṛttikābhyo namaḥ".
Endowment given after Plantation – gave **gold** earrings to a young lady.

Gular Tree with a pair of bulbul.

9th Day 2-04-2025 Evening Rohini - Jamun

PLANTATION DAY 9. Evening.
Date: Wednesday 2-04-2025, 5 – 6:15 pm, Pancami Tithi.
Nakshatra Birth Star: 4. रोहिणी Rohini - Aldebaran
Constellation: Taurus (Zodiac).

Sacred Tree Planted (4 nos):
जामुन jamun = black plum – syzygium cuminii

Sacred Mantra – "oṃ rohiṇyai namaḥ".
Endowment given after Plantation – gave a jar of cow-**ghee** to an office boy.

Jamun Tree

10th Day 3-04-2025 Mrigashira - Khadir

PLANTATION DAY 10. Morning.
Date: Thursday 3-04-2025, 8 – 9:30 am, Shasthi Tithi.
Nakshatra Birth Star: 5. मृगशिरा Mrigashira – λ Orionis = Meissa
Constellation: Orion (Zodiac).

Sacred Tree Planted (4 nos):
खदिर khadir = cutch – acacia catechu

Sacred Mantra – "oṃ mṛgaśīrṣāya namaḥ".
Endowment given after Plantation – gave **sesame**-laddu to a maid.

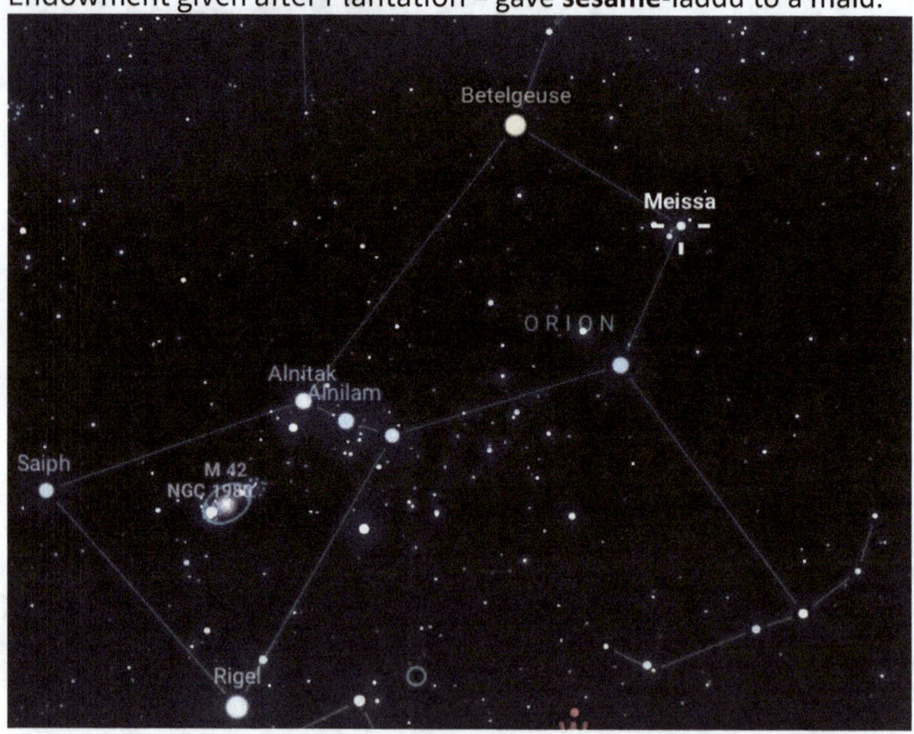

Khadir Tree. Rare and Costly.

11th Day 4-04-2025 Ardra - Red Sandalwood

PLANTATION DAY 11. Morning.
Date: Friday 4-04-2025, 7:45 – 9:15 am, Saptami Tithi.
Nakshatra Birth Star: 6. आर्द्रा Ardra - Betelgeuse
Constellation: Orion (Zodiac).

Sacred Tree Planted (4 nos):
कृष्णगुरु krishnaguru = red sandalwood – pterocarpus santalinus

Sacred Mantra – "oṃ ārdrāyai namaḥ".

Endowment given after Plantation – gave a milking sahiwal **desi cow** with calf to office road-cleaning-machine operator.

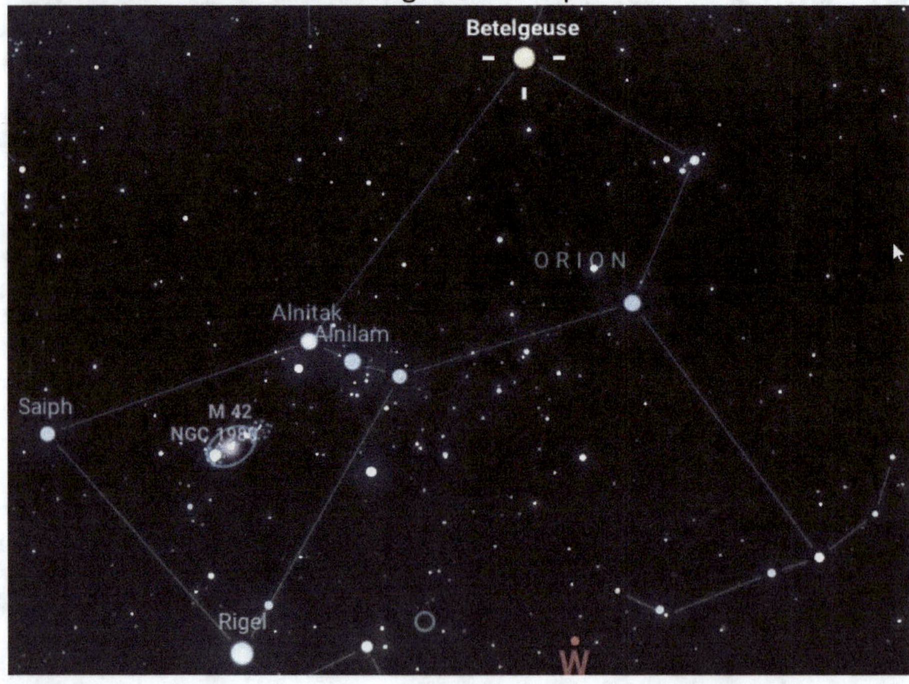

Red Sandalwood Tree.

12th Day 5-04-2025 Punarvasu - Bamboo

PLANTATION DAY 12. Evening.
Date: Saturday 5-04-2025, 5 – 6:15 pm, Ashtami Tithi.
Nakshatra Birth Star: 7. पुनर्वसु Punarvasu – Castor & Pollux
Constellation: Gemini (Zodiac).

Sacred Tree Planted (4 nos):
बांस baans = bamboo – bambusa vulgaris

Sacred Mantra – "oṃ punarvasubhyāṃ namaḥ".

Endowment given after Plantation – gave a **brass** item to a maid.

Bamboo Saplings.

13th Day 6-04-2025 Pushya - Peepal

PLANTATION DAY 13. Morning.
Date: Sunday 6-04-2025, 7:45 – 9:15 am, Navami Tithi.
Nakshatra Birth Star: 8. पुष्य Pushya - Asellus Australis = δ Cancri
Constellation: Cancer (Zodiac).

Sacred Tree Planted (4 nos):
पीपल peepal = sacred fig – ficus religiosa

Sacred Mantra – "oṃ puṣyāya namaḥ".

Endowment given after Plantation – fed **breakfast with sesame-laddu** to security-guard.

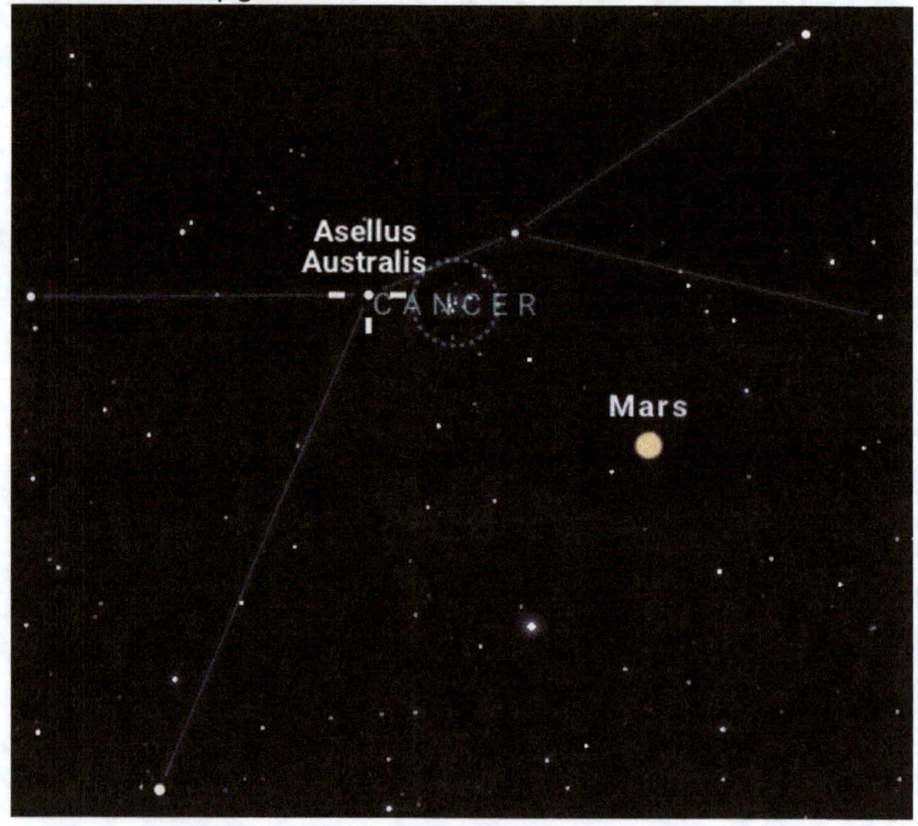

14th Day 7-04-2025 Ashlesha - Nag Champa

PLANTATION DAY 14. Morning.
Date: Monday 7-04-2025, 7:45 – 9:15 am, Dashami Tithi.
Nakshatra Birth Star: 9. आश्लेषा Ashlesha - δ Hydrae.
Constellation: Hydra.
Sacred Tree: नागचम्पा nag champa =bridal bouquet–plumeria pudica
Sacred Mantra – "oṃ āśleṣāyai namaḥ".

Endowment given after Plantation - gave a milking sahiwal **desi cow** with calf to lady living opposite.

Nag Champa Tree.

15th Day 8-04-2025 Magha - Banyan

PLANTATION DAY 15. Morning.
Date: Tuesday 8-04-2025, 8:30 – 9:45 am, Ekadashi Tithi.
Nakshatra Birth Star: 10. मघा Magha - Regulus
Constellation: Leo (Zodiac).

Sacred Tree Planted (4 nos):
बरगद bargad = banyan – ficus benghalensis

Sacred Mantra – "oṃ maghāyai namaḥ".

Endowment given after Plantation - gave a milking sahiwal **desi cow** to friend of office help.

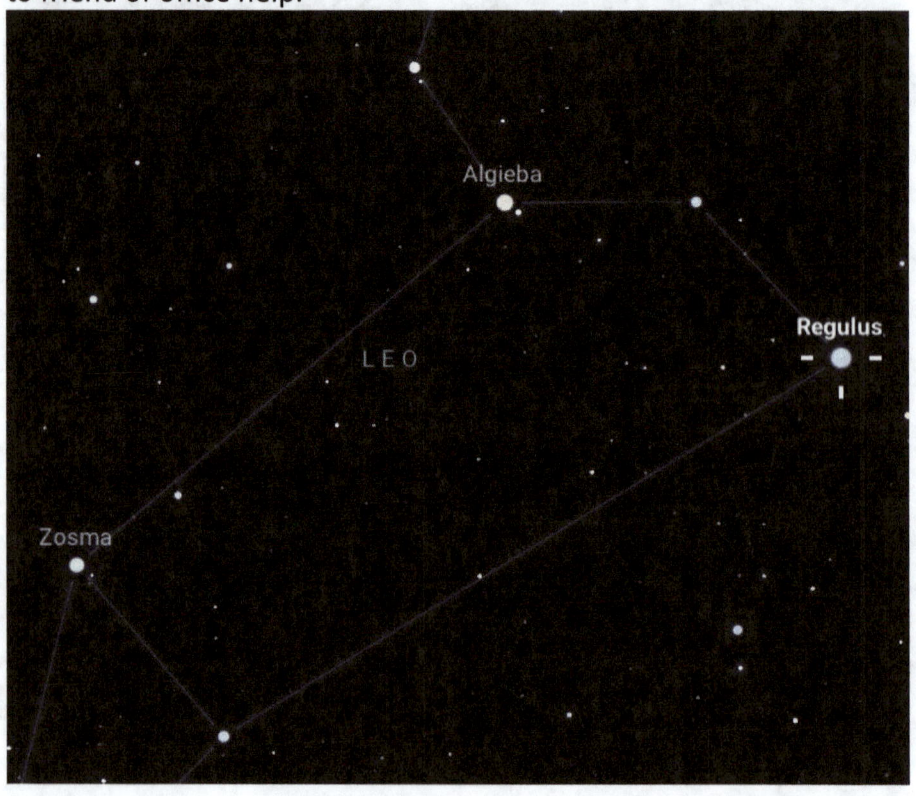

Banyan Trees in front of Krishna Temple.

16th Day 9-04-2025 P. Phalguni - Palash

PLANTATION DAY 16. Evening.
Date: Wednesday 9-04-2025, 5 – 6:15 pm, Dvadashi Tithi.
Nakshatra Star: 11. पूर्वा फाल्गुनी Purva Phalguni - δ Leonis = Zosma
Constellation: Leo (Zodiac).

Sacred Tree Planted (4 nos):
पलाश palash = flame of the forest – butea monosperma

Sacred Mantra – "oṃ pūrvā phālgunībhyāṃ namaḥ".
Endowment given after Plantation - fed **dinner** to a maid.

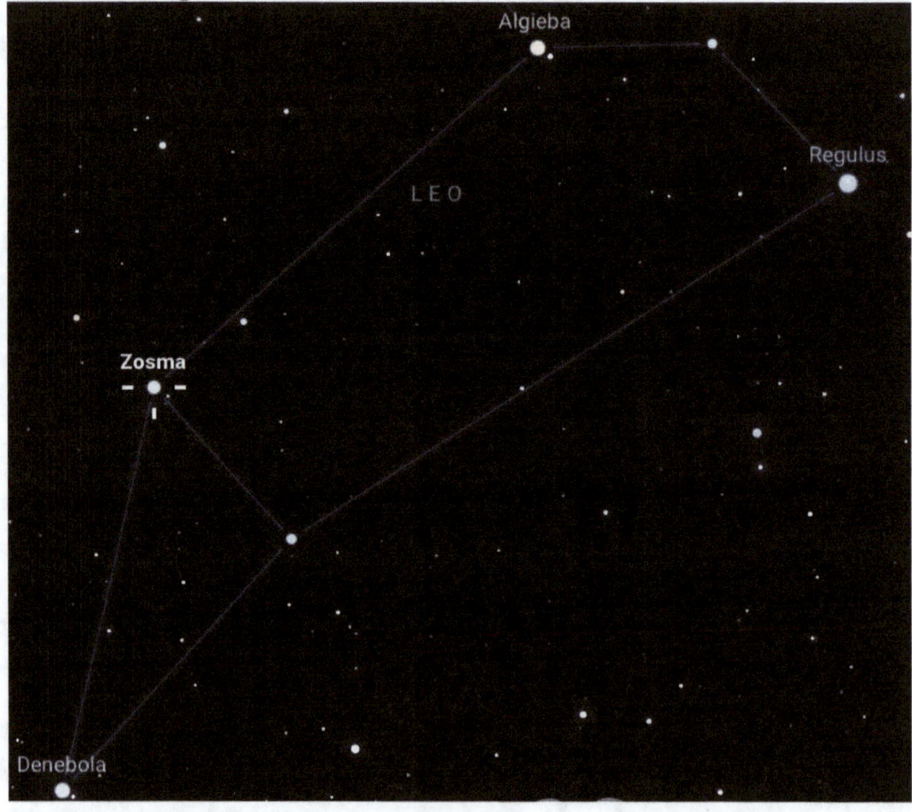

Palash Tree some distance from Krishna Temple land.

17ᵗʰ Day 10-04-2025 U. Phalguni - Paakad

PLANTATION DAY 17. Evening.
Date: Thursday 10-04-2025, 5 – 6:15 pm, Trayodashi Tithi.
Nakshatra Birth Star: 12. उत्तरा फाल्गुनी Uttara Phalguni - Denebola
Constellation: Leo (Zodiac).

Sacred Tree Planted (4 nos):
पाकड paakad = java fig – ficus lacor

Sacred Mantra – "oṃ uttarā phālgunībhyāṃ namaḥ".
Endowment given after Plantation - fed **dinner** to an office help.

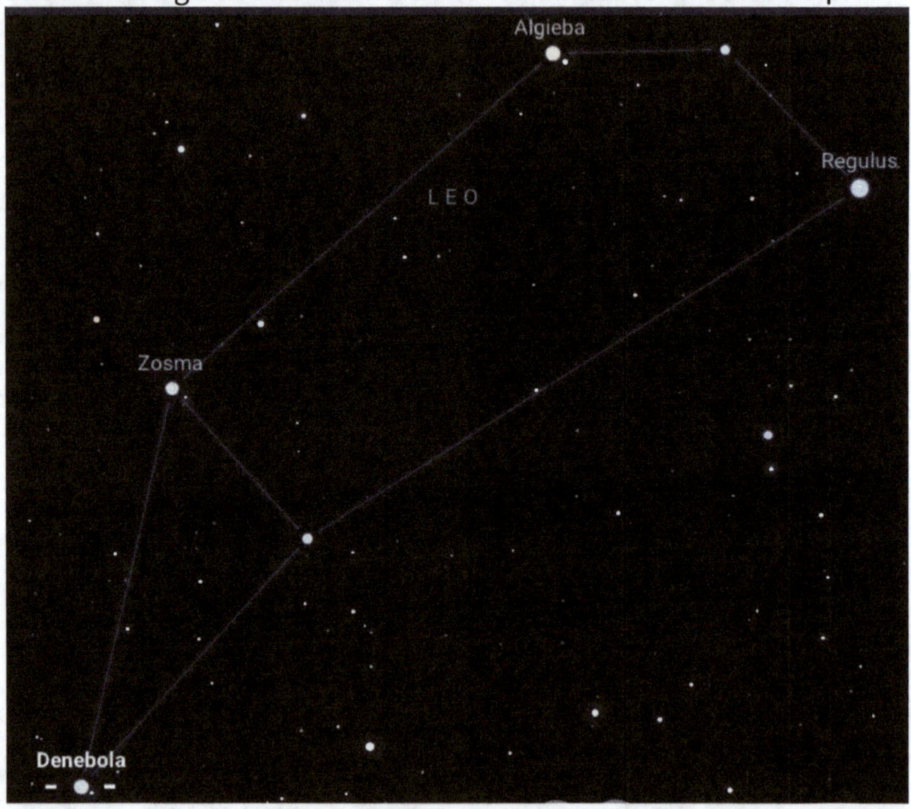

Paakad Sapling along road facing North Exit.

PLANTATION DAY 18. Evening.
Date: Friday 11-04-2025, 5 – 6:15 pm, Chaturdashi Tithi.
Nakshatra Birth Star: 13. हस्त Hasta - β Corvi = Kraz
Constellation: Corvus.

Sacred Tree Planted (4 nos):
जूही juhi = jasmine – jasminum auriculatum

Sacred Mantra – "oṃ hastāya namaḥ".
Endowment given after Plantation - fed **dinner** to a security guard.

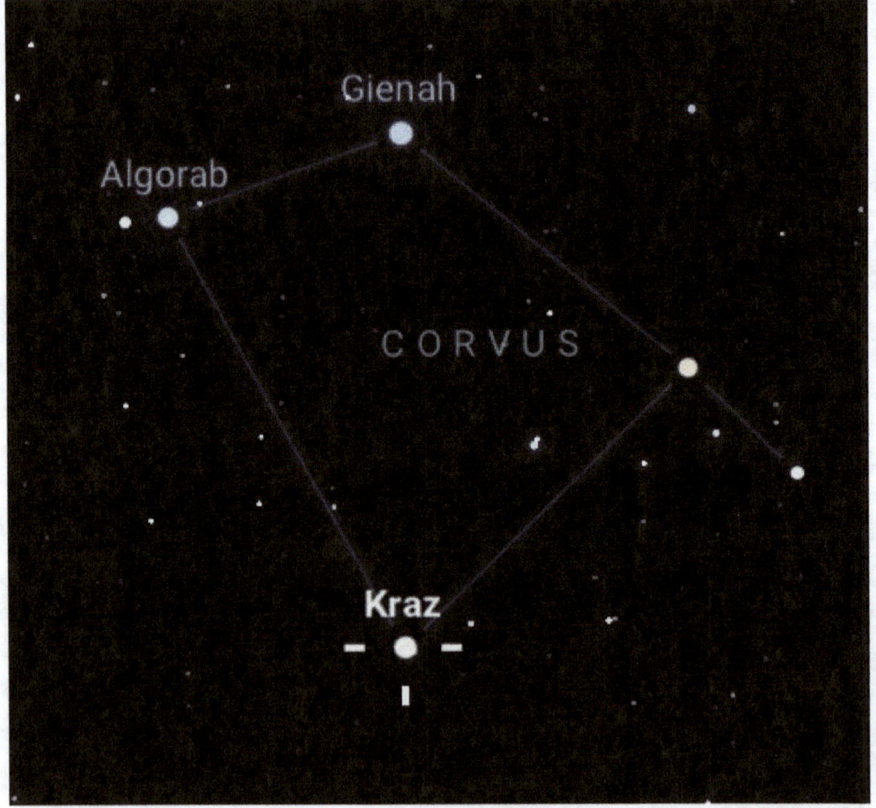

Juhi Sapling.

19th Day 12-04-2025 Chitra - Bel Patra

PLANTATION DAY 19. Evening.
Date: Saturday 12-04-2025, 6:30 – 7:45 pm, Chaitra **Poornima** Tithi.
Hanuman Jayanti.
Nakshatra Birth Star: 14. चित्रा Chitra - Spica
Constellation: Virgo (Zodiac).

Sacred Tree Planted (4 nos):
बेल पत्र bel-patra = wood apple – aegle marmelos

Sacred Mantra – "oṃ citrāyai namaḥ".

Endowment given after Plantation – offered **milk** bottles to sadhus at Dandi Swami Mandir.

Bel Patra Sapling.

20th Day 13-04-2025 Skipped

Lord Sri **Krishna Temple** Foundation Stone laid. 7 – 9 am, in the Nakshatra Van adjacent area. Directors with families, Architect, Civil Engineer, Mason, all teammates present. Faces correct EAST

Foundation Stone in NE Corner with Pancadhatu and 16 Bricks.

    1. Sri Sri

    2. Ashwini

    3. Mother

    4. Jagjit

    5. Amroz

    6. Manu and 7. Gitanjali

    8. Alok Kathuria (Architect)

    9. Ravinder Singh Bedi (Civil Engineer)

    10. Bhavleen

    11. Kamaljit (Kiran)

    12. Mason

    13. Sameer

    14. Kyan

    15. Narinder (Site Supervisor) 16. Charanjeet (Chief Secretary)

Skipped Tree Plantation on this day.

21ˢᵗ Day 14-04-2025 Svati - Arjun

PLANTATION DAY 21.
Date: Monday 14-04-2025, 7:45 – 9:15 am, Pratipada Tithi.
Nakshatra Birth Star: 15. स्वाति Svati - Arcturus
Constellation: Bootes.

Sacred Tree Planted (4 nos):
अर्जुन arjun = arjuna – terminalia arjuna

Sacred Mantra – "oṃ svātyai namaḥ".

Endowment given after Plantation – gave 10kg **cow ghee** to baba Sajjan-ji-da-khoo gurudwara.

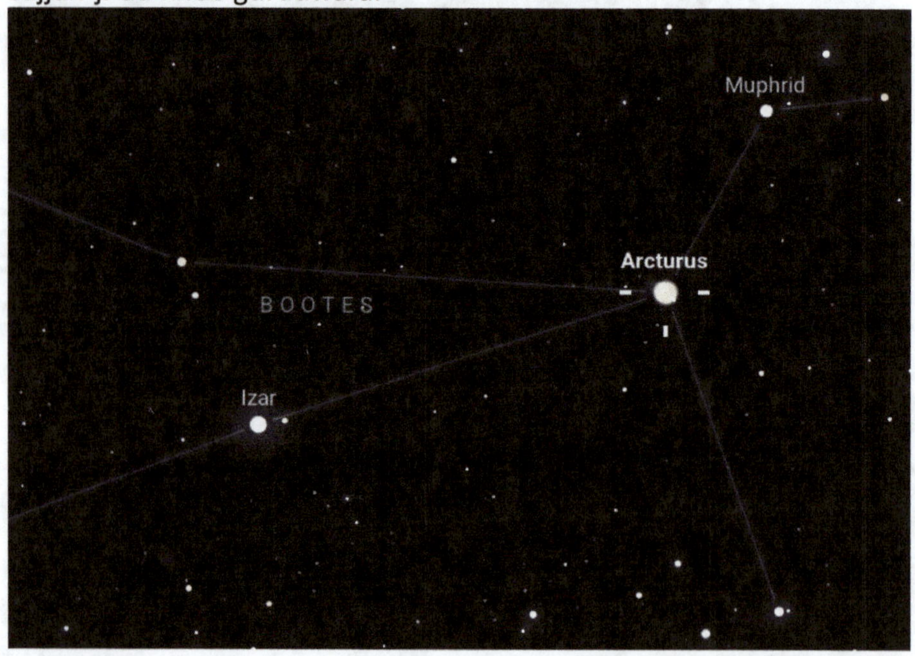

Arjun Trees.

22nd Day 15-04-2025 Vishakha - Vikankat

PLANTATION DAY 22.
Date: Tuesday 15-04-2025, 7:45 – 9:15 am, Dvitiya Tithi.
Nakshatra Birth Star: 16. विशाखा Vishakha - Zubeneschamali
Constellation: Libra (Zodiac).

Sacred Tree Planted (4 nos):
विकंकत vikankat = governor's plum – flacourtia indica

Sacred Mantra – "oṃ viśākhābhyāṃ namaḥ".

Endowment given after Plantation - gave 10kg **cow ghee** to Nanaksar gurudwara opposite PAU campus.

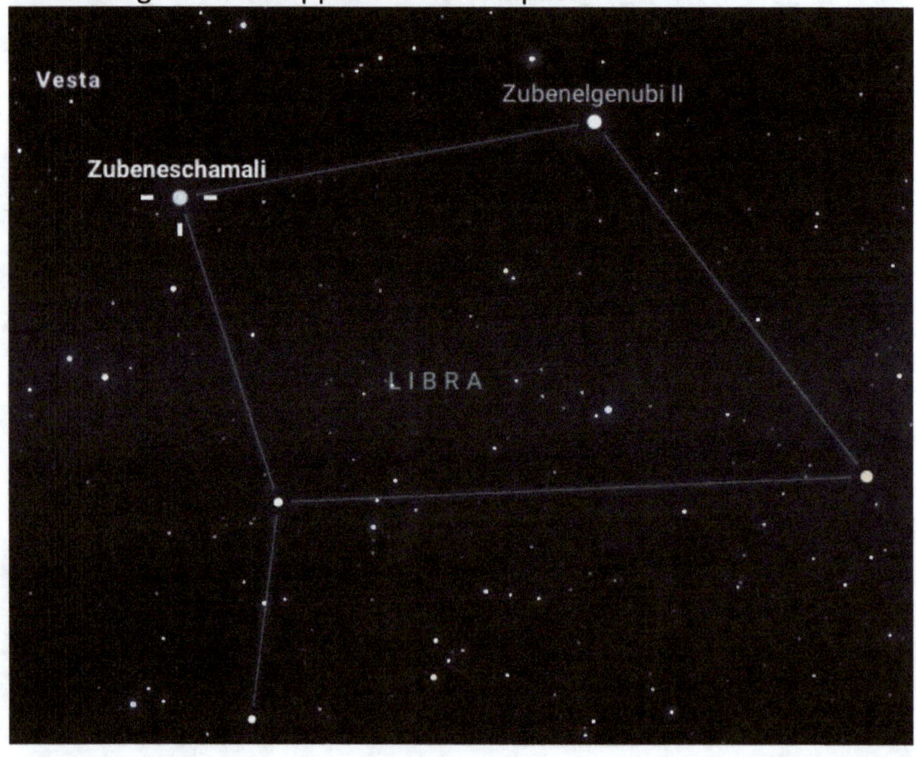

Vikankat Sapling.

23rd Day 16-04-2025 Anuradha - Maulshree

PLANTATION DAY 23.
Date: Wednesday 16-04-2025, 7:45 – 9:15 am, Tritiya Tithi.
Nakshatra Birth Star: 17. अनुराधा Anuradha – Dschubba = δ Scorpii
Constellation: Scorpius (Zodiac).

Sacred Tree Planted (4 nos):
मौलश्री maulshree = spanish cherry – mimusops elengi

Sacred Mantra – "oṃ anurādhābhyo namaḥ".

Endowment given after Plantation - gave 10kg **cow ghee** to Alamgir gurudwara.

Aarti after planting Maulshree Tree. 9:07 AM

24th Day 17-04-2025 Jyeshtha - Semal

PLANTATION DAY 24.
Date: Thursday 17-04-2025, 7:45 – 9:15 am, Chaturthi Tithi.
Nakshatra Birth Star: 18. ज्येष्ठा Jyeshtha - Antares
Constellation: Scorpius (Zodiac).

Sacred Tree Planted (4 nos):
सेमल semal = silk cotton – bombax ceiba

Sacred Mantra – "oṃ jyeṣṭhāyai namaḥ".

Endowment given after Plantation – gave **sesame**-laddu to den help.

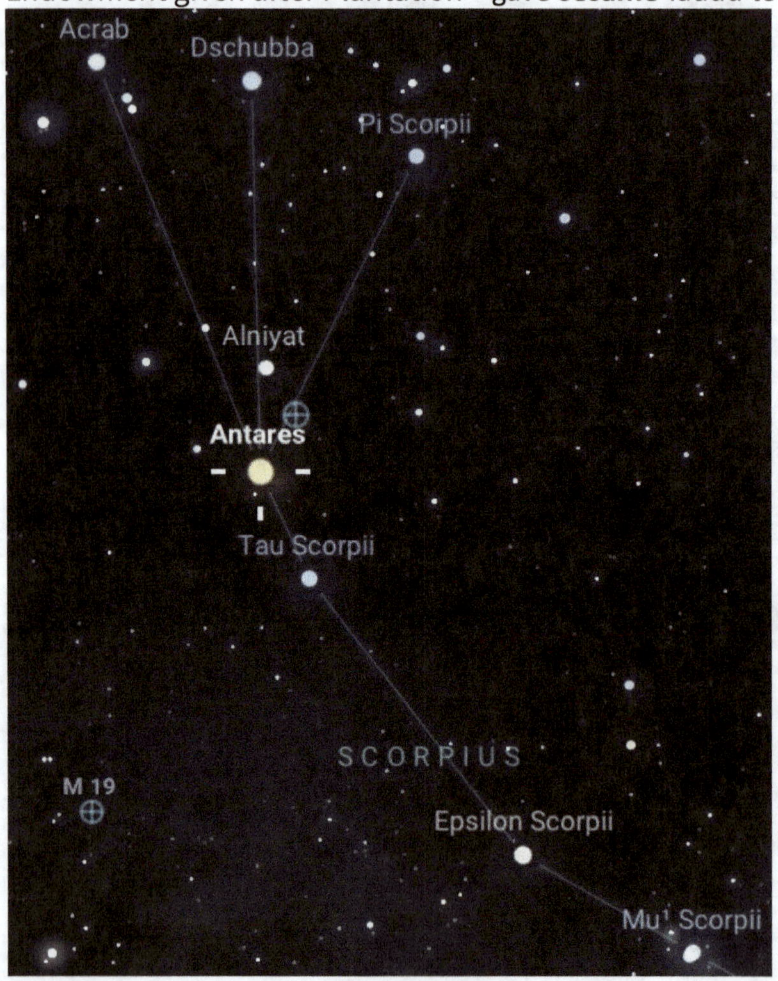

Semal

25th Day 18-04-2025 Mula - Sal

PLANTATION DAY 25. Greeted by strong winds. Light rain drops.
Date: Friday 18-04-2025, 5 – 6:15 pm, Pancami Tithi.
Nakshatra Birth Star: 19. मूल Mula – λ Scorpii = Shaula
Constellation: Scorpius (Zodiac).
Sacred Tree Planted (4 nos):

राल, साल sal = common sal – shorea robusta gaertn

Sacred Mantra – "oṃ mūlāya namaḥ".

Endowment given after Plantation – gave a **silver** tumbler to cosmo club-in charge.

Sal Tree

26th Day 19-04-2025 P. Ashadha - Slender Rattan Cane

PLANTATION DAY 26. Though the sun was right overhead, the weather was nice and comfortable.

Date: Saturday 19-04-2025, 11 am – 12:15 pm noon, Shasthi Tithi.
Nakshatra Birth Star: 20. पूर्वा आषाढा Purva Ashadha - Kaus Australis
Constellation: Sagittarius (Zodiac).

Sacred Tree Planted (4 nos):
वेंत vaint = slender rattan cane – calamus pseudotenuis

Sacred Mantra – "oṃ pūrvāṣāḍhābhyāṃ namaḥ".

Endowment given after Plantation - gave a milking sahiwal **desi cow** to relative lady of dadu.

Slender Rattan Cane (with thorns)

27th Day 21-04-2025 U. Ashadha - Jackfruit

PLANTATION DAY 27.
Date: Monday 21-04-2025, 7:45 – 9:15 am, Ashtami Tithi.
Nakshatra Birth Star: 21. उत्तरा आषाढा Uttara Ashadha - Nunki
Constellation: Sagittarius (Zodiac).

Sacred Tree Planted (4 nos):
कटहल kathal = jackfruit – artocarpus heterophyllus

Sacred Mantra – "oṃ uttarāṣāḍhābhyāṃ namaḥ".
Endowment given after Plantation - fed **breakfast** to all members of our garden plantation team.

Jackfruit Tree

Moon's Movement along Elliptic East to West

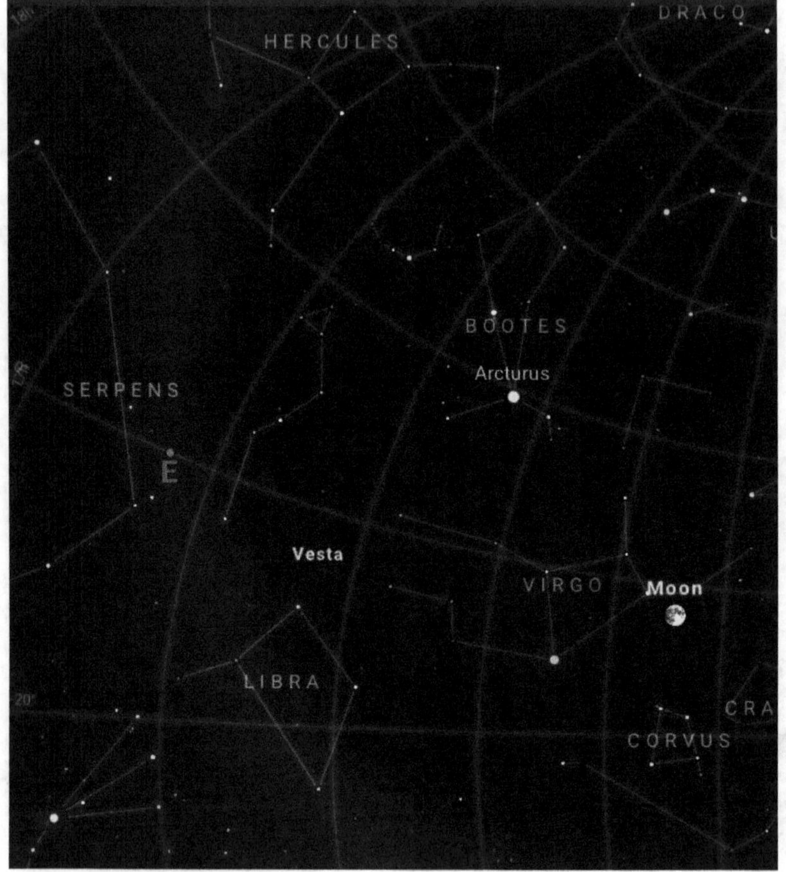

As on 11 April 2025, 9pm.

Moon's Movement … East to West

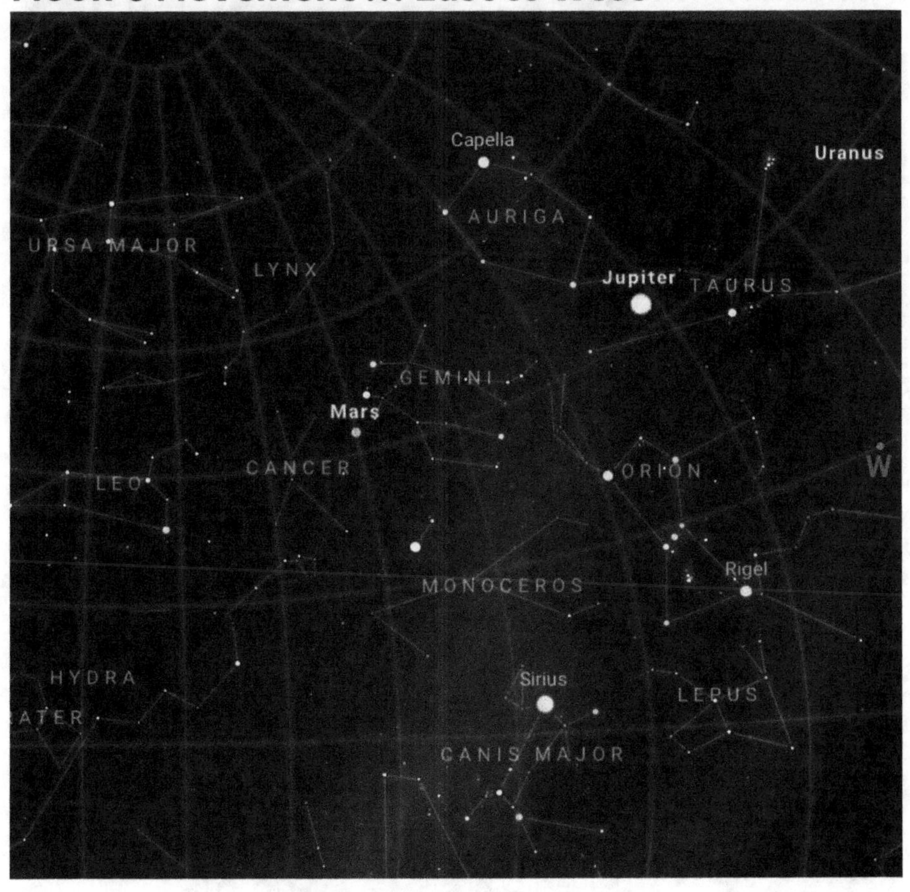

25th March

PUJA TENT

Sahiwal Milking Desi Cow with Calf. 4th April

Papa Birthday after Nag Champa Tree Plantation 7th April

16th April Maulshree Tree

16th April Maulshree Tree

21st April. Final Day Puja.

21st April. Final Day.

Maps Location

<https://maps.app.goo.gl/BniZ4CXLz8iTr6s39>

Sun View Residency. Near North Exit.

The Nakshatra Van site is 2 acres in size approx.

108 Trees of 27 types for 27 Nakshatra planted from 25 Mar to 21 Apr 2025.

N
NW
NE
W
E
SW
SE
S

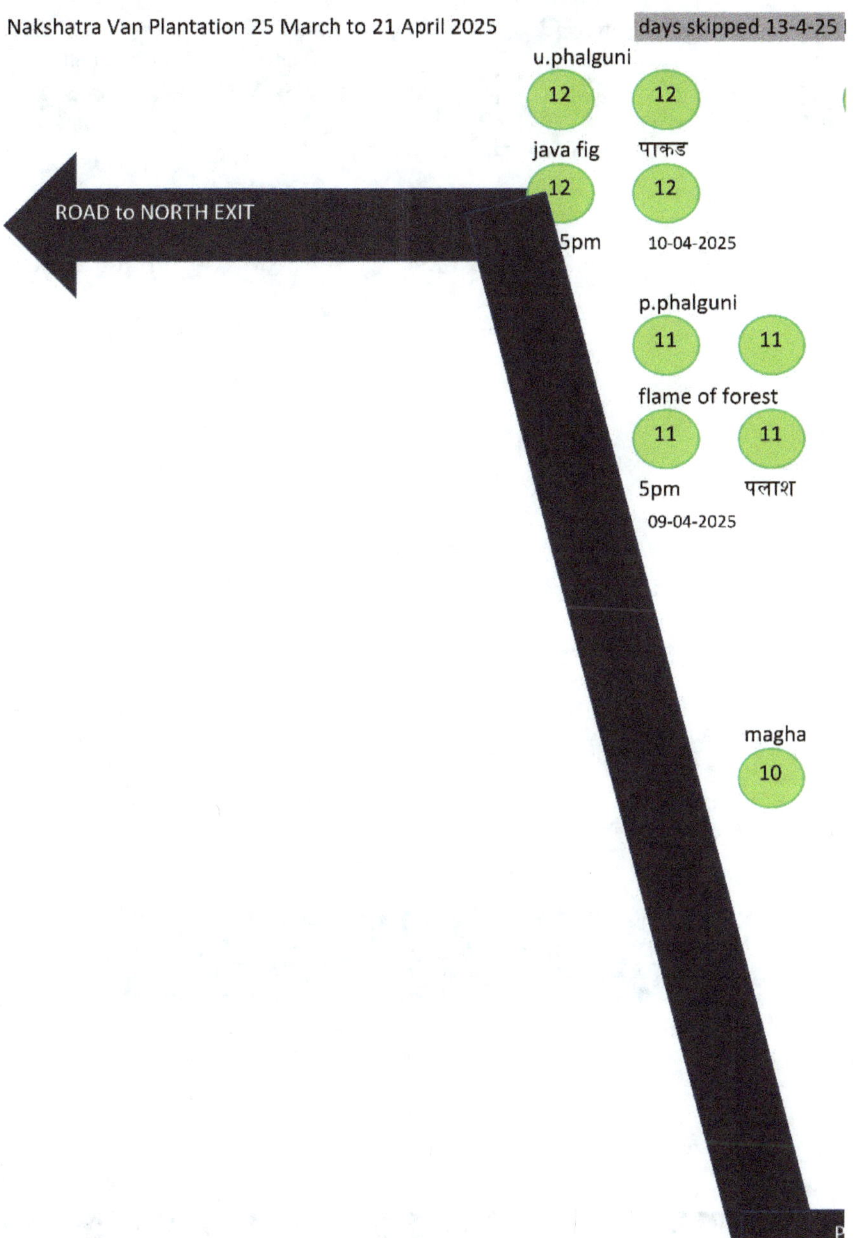
days skipped 13-4-25
u.phalguni
12
12
java fig
पाकड
12
12
5pm
10-04-2025
p.phalguni
11
11
flame of forest
11
11
5pm
पलाश
09-04-2025
magha
10
ROAD to NORTH EXIT

Baisakhi, 20-4-25 Sthapati
hasta
5pm
chitra
6:30pm
13
13
13
13
14
14
14
jasmine
11-04-2025 जूही
wood apple
12-04-2025

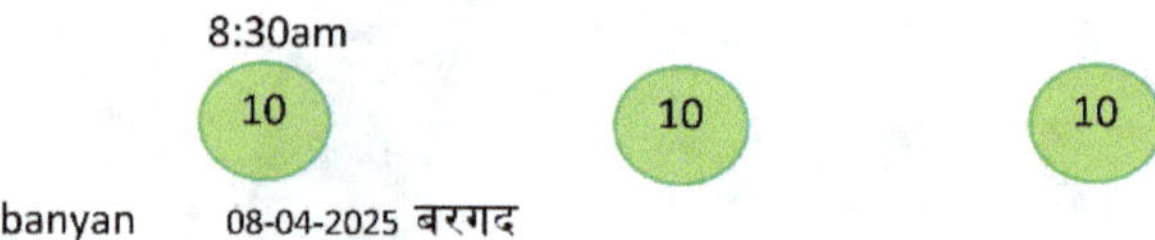

8:30am
10
10
10
banyan
08-04-2025 बरगद

LORD SRI KRISHNA TEMPLE
13-4-25 Baisakhi foundation stone laid with group Havan
20-4-25 measurements 50'x100' by Sthapati

PLOT BOUNDARY / ROAD to SRI YANTRA Pillar

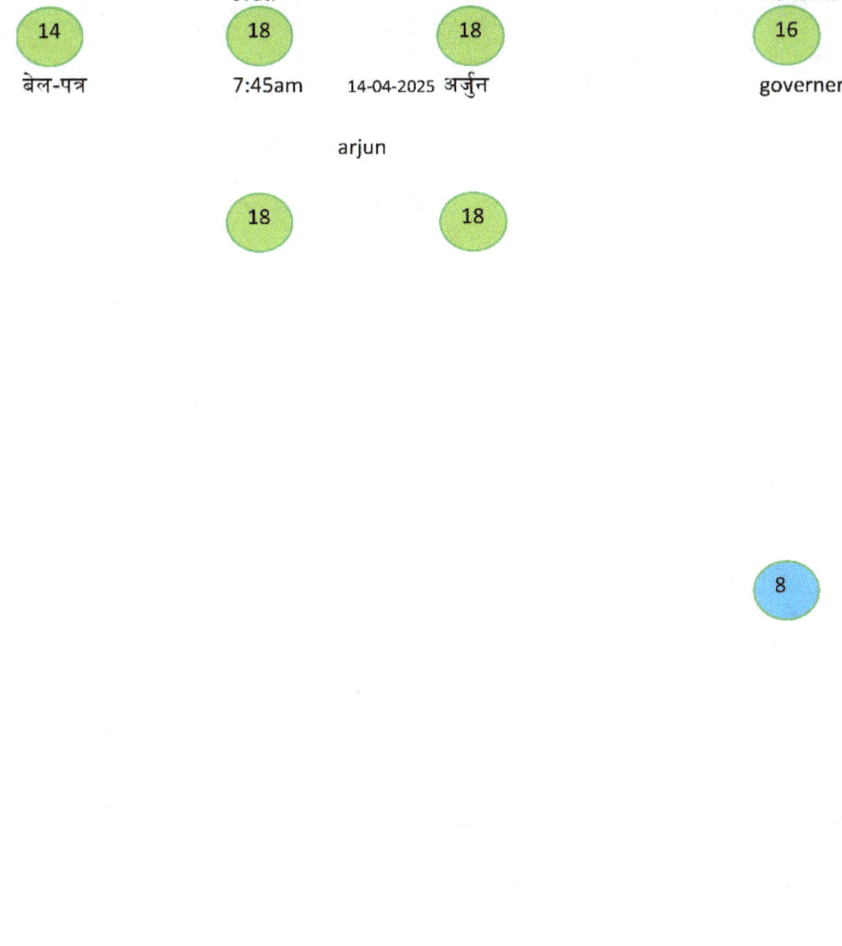

svati
14
18
18
बेल-पत्र
7:45am
14-04-2025
अर्जुन
vishakha
16
governer's
arjun
18
18
8
7:45am
bridal bouquet
ashlesha
07-04-2025
नागचम्पा
9
9
9
9
8
PAPA's Birthday celebrated with cow daan

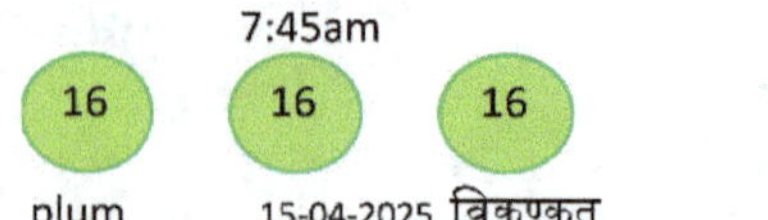

PHOTOGRAPHY DAY
Trees 18 to 21 are not present
as these were not planted yet.

8

sacred fig

7   7   6

pushya   punarvasu   ardra

7:45am   5pm   7:45am
06-04-2025   05-04-2025   04-04-2025

पीपल   bamboo   बांस   red sandal
8   7   7   6

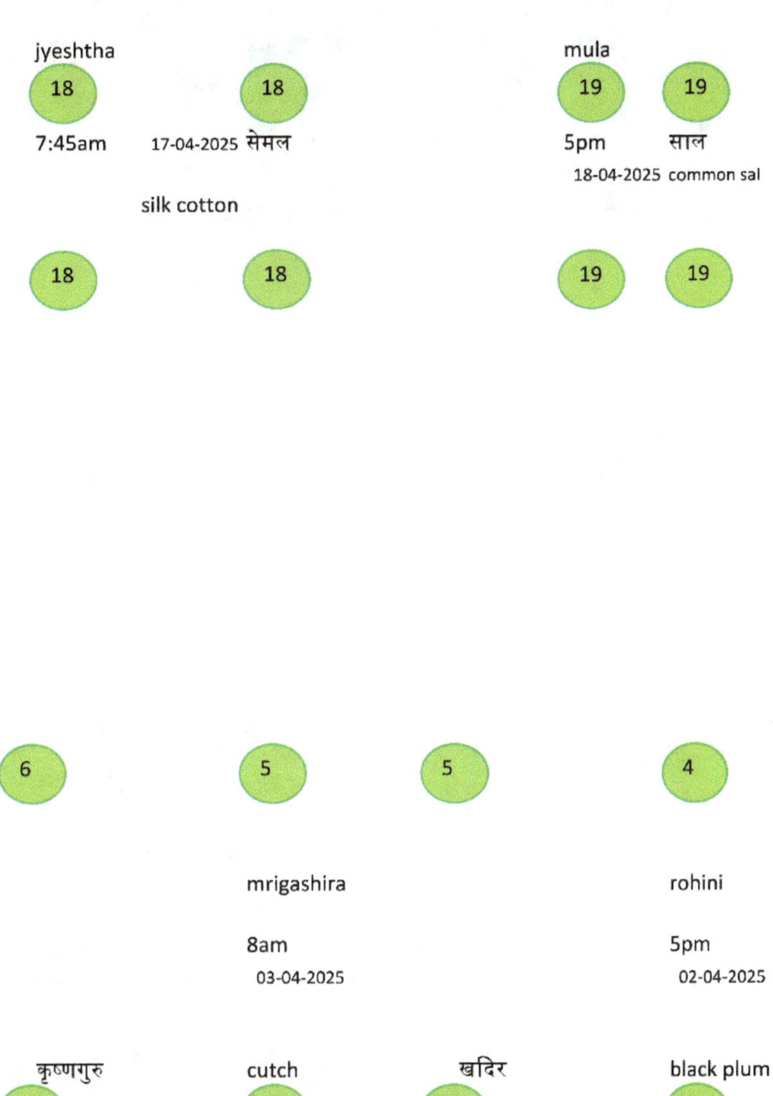

jyeshtha
18
18
7:45am
17-04-2025
सेमल
silk cotton
18
18
mula
19
19
5pm
साल
18-04-2025
common sal
19
19
6
5
5
4
mrigashira
rohini
8am
5pm
03-04-2025
02-04-2025
कृष्णगुरु
cutch
खदिर
black plum
6
5
5
4

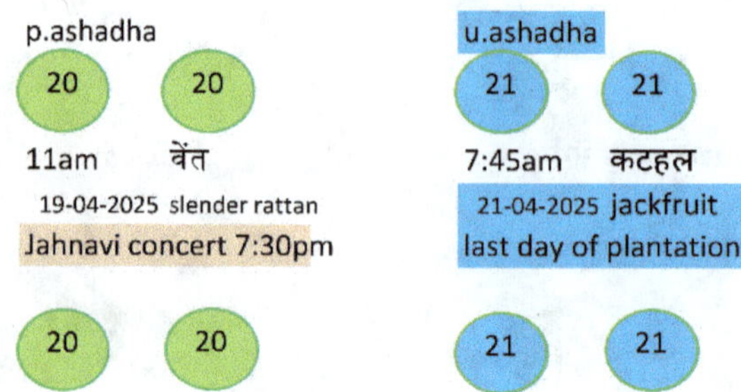

p.ashadha
20
20
11am
बेंत
19-04-2025 slender rattan
Jahnavi concert 7:30pm
20
20
u.ashadha
21
21
7:45am
कटहल
21-04-2025 jackfruit
last day of plantation
21
21

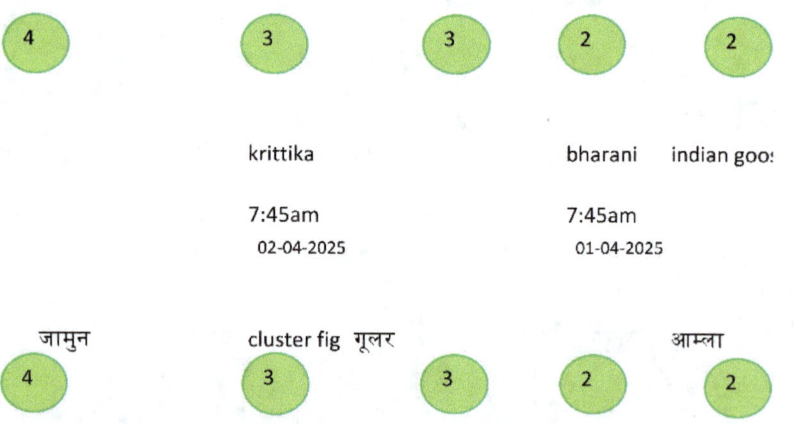

4
3
3
2
2
krittika
bharani   indian goo:
7:45am
7:45am
02-04-2025
01-04-2025
जामुन
cluster fig गूलर
आम्ला
4
3
3
2
2

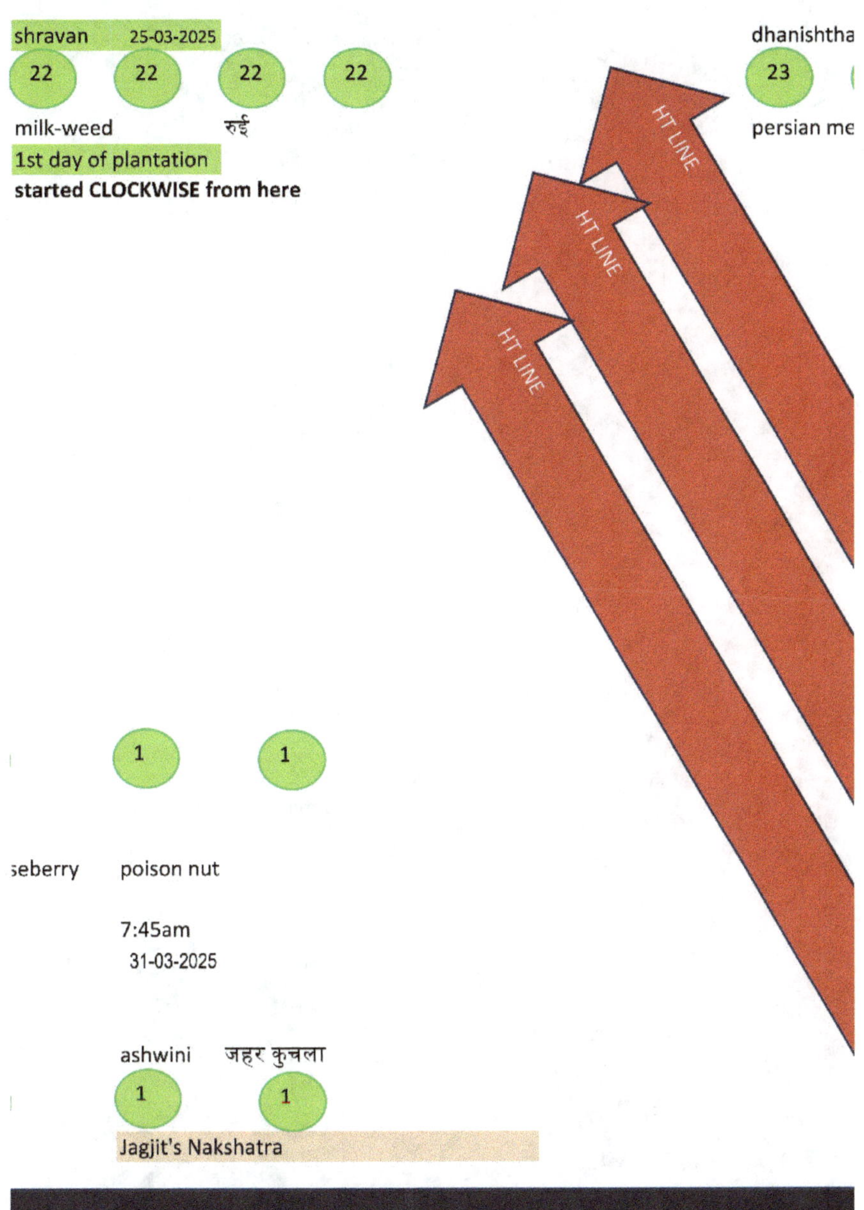

shravan	25-03-2025
22	22	22	22
milk-weed	रुई
1st day of plantation
started CLOCKWISE from here
dhanishtha
23
persian me
HT LINE
HT LINE
HT LINE
1	1
seberry	poison nut
7:45am
31-03-2025
ashwini	जहर कुचला
1	1
Jagjit's Nakshatra

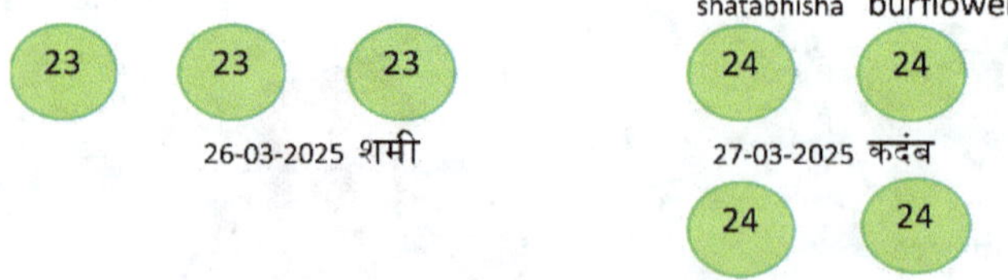

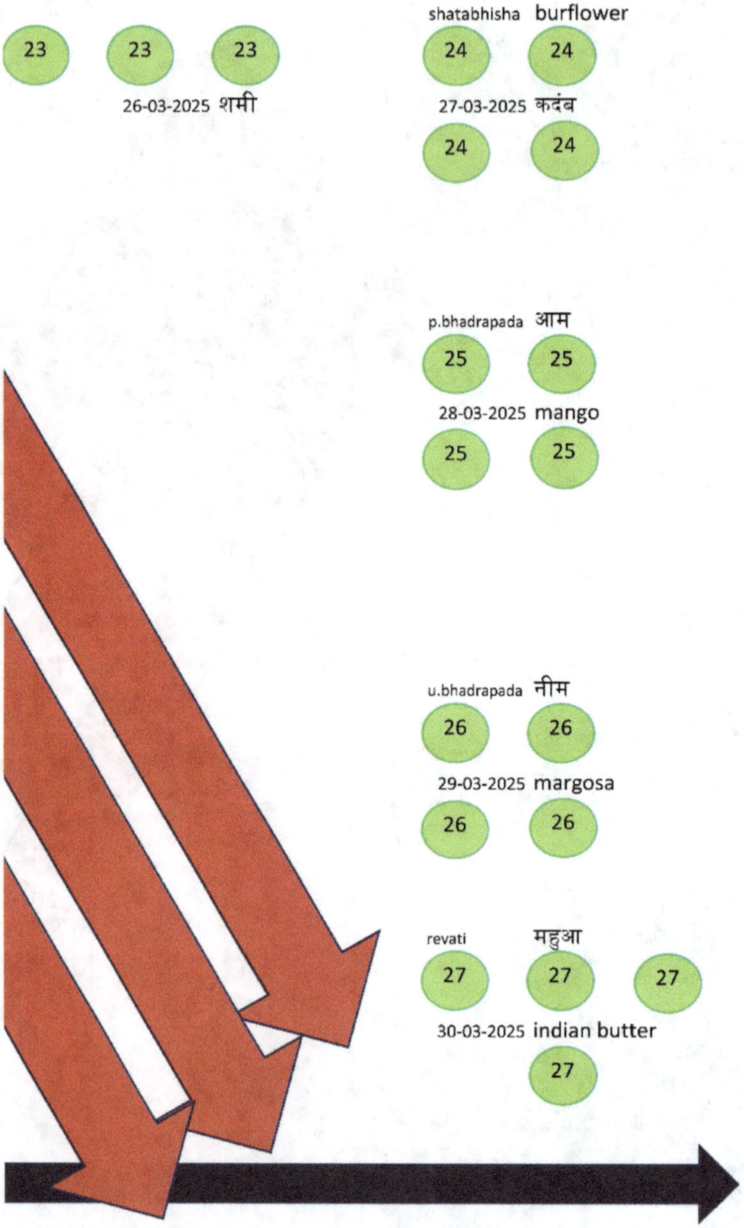

23
23
23
26-03-2025 शमी
shatabhisha burflower
24
24
27-03-2025 कदंब
24
24
p.bhadrapada आम
25
25
28-03-2025 mango
25
25
u.bhadrapada नीम
26
26
29-03-2025 margosa
26
26
revati महुआ
27
27
27
30-03-2025 indian butter
27

Verses to invoke Auspiciousness

oṃ svastiḥ prajābhyaᕁ paripālayantām | nyāyena mārgeṇa mahīṃ
mahīśāḥ | go brāhmaṇebhyaḥ śubhamastu nityam |
lokāḥ samastāḥ sukhino bhavantu ||
kāle varṣatu parjanyaḥ pṛthivī sasyaśālinī |
deśo'yaṃ kṣobharahitaḥ brāhmaṇāḥ santu nirbhayāḥ ||

<u>Aashir Vacanam</u>
sarve bhavantu sukhinaḥ | sarve santu nirāmayāḥ |
sarve bhadrāṇi paśyantu | mā kaścid duḥkhabhāg bhavet ||

asato mā sad gamaya |
tamaso mā jyotir gamaya |
mṛtyor mā amṛtaṃ gamaya ||

oṃ pūrṇamadaḥ pūrṇamidaṃ pūrṇāt pūrṇamudacyate |
pūrṇasya pūrṇamādāya pūrṇamevāvaśiṣyate ||

|| oṃ śāntiḥ śāntiḥ śāntiḥ ||

Index

Star Gazing

Nakshatra Stars we actually saw in the night along with the Moon.
25-03-2025 Shravan - Altair
31-03-2025 Ashwini – Sheratan
1-04-2025 Krittika - Pleiades
2-04-2025 Rohini - Aldebaran
3-04-2025 Mrigashira - Meissa
4-04-2025 Ardra - Betelgeuse
5-04-2025 Punarvasu - Castor and Pollux
11-04-2025 Hasta – Kraz
12-04-2025 Chitra - Spica
14-04-2025 Svati – Arcturus
17-04-2025 Jyeshtha – Antares

Epilogue

सर्वे भवन्तु सुखिनः । सर्वे सन्तु निरामयाः ।
सर्वे भद्राणि पश्यन्तु । मा कश्चिद् दुःख भाग् भवेत् ॥
ॐ शान्तिः शान्तिः शान्तिः ॥

When faith has blossomed in life, Every step is led by the Divine.

Sri Sri Ravi Shankar

Om Namah Shivaya

जय गुरुदेव